High-Stakes Careers

FIGHTER PILOTS

Trudy Becker

WWW.APEXEDITIONS.COM

Copyright © 2026 by Apex Editions, Mendota Heights, MN 55120. All rights reserved. No part of this book may be reproduced or utilized in any form or by any means without written permission from the publisher.

Apex is distributed by North Star Editions:
sales@northstareditions.com | 888-417-0195

Produced for Apex by Red Line Editorial.

Photographs ©: Shutterstock Images, cover, 1, 10–11, 18–19, 22–23, 24–25, 26–27, 34–35, 36–37, 38–39, 44–45, 54–55; Tech. Sgt. Adam Keele/US Air National Guard/DVIDS, 4–5; Master Sgt. Michael Jackson/DVIDS, 6–7; Japan Air Self-Defense Force/AP Images, 8–9; Jerod Harris/Getty Images News/Getty Images, 12–13; Athanasios Gioumpasis/Getty Images News/Getty Images, 14–15; Joint Staff Office of the Defense Ministry of Japan/AP Images, 16–17; Mass Communication Specialist Second Class Justin A. Johndro/US Navy/DVIDS, 20–21; Senior Airman Zachary Willis/US Air Force/DVIDS, 29, 58; South Korean Defense Ministry/Getty Images News/Getty Images, 30–31; Corbis Historical/Getty Images, 32–33; Greg Mathieson/Mai/The Chronicle Collection/Getty Images, 41; Senior Airman Jack Rodgers/US Air Force/DVIDS, 42–43; Libkos/Getty Images News/Getty Images, 46–47; Alain Nogues/Sygma/Getty Images, 48–49; Justin Pacheco/US Air Force/DVIDS, 50–51; Sean M. Worrell/US Air Force/DVIDS, 52–53; Airman 1st Class Katelynn Jackson/US Air Force/DVIDS, 56–57

Library of Congress Control Number: 2025930336

ISBN
979-8-89250-670-0 (hardcover)
979-8-89250-704-2 (ebook pdf)
979-8-89250-688-5 (hosted ebook)

Printed in the United States of America
Mankato, MN
082025

NOTE TO PARENTS AND EDUCATORS

Apex books are designed to build literacy skills in striving readers. Exciting, high-interest content attracts and holds readers' attention. The text is carefully leveled to allow students to achieve success quickly.

TABLE OF CONTENTS

Chapter 1
SKY FIGHT 4

Chapter 2
WHAT ARE FIGHTER PILOTS? 9

Chapter 3
AIR TO AIR 18

Story Spotlight
DOWNING DRONES 28

Chapter 4
AIR TO GROUND 30

Story Spotlight
DESERT STORM 40

Chapter 5
RISKS AND CHALLENGES 42

Chapter 6
TRAINING 50

SKILLS CHECKLIST • 59
COMPREHENSION QUESTIONS • 60
GLOSSARY • 62
TO LEARN MORE • 63
ABOUT THE AUTHOR • 63
INDEX • 64

Chapter 1
SKY FIGHT

A fighter pilot zooms through the air. Her jet glides high above mountains. Suddenly, a mark appears on her display screen. Her jet's radar has found something. An enemy plane is chasing her.

The F-35 Lightning II is used by militaries in several countries. The jet can fly 50,000 feet (15,240 m) above the ground.

Some missiles travel more than 3,000 miles per hour (4,830 km/h).

The fighter pilot weaves through the air. She dips and zigzags. The enemy plane fires a missile. But the fighter pilot dodges it. She zooms higher into the air. Then she turns and fires her own missiles. They hit the enemy plane. It bursts into flames.

TRACKING TARGETS

Fighter jets often shoot heat-seeking weapons. The weapons can sense heat. This helps them find and hit targets. For example, some missiles can detect exhaust from jet engines. They fly toward it. This helps them hit planes.

Navy fighter jets may protect ships from enemy planes.

Chapter 2
WHAT ARE FIGHTER PILOTS?

Fighter pilots work for militaries around the world. Many serve in a country's air force. But they can be part of other military branches. For example, many navies have fighter pilots. So does the US Marine Corps.

Fighter pilots fly airplanes called fighter jets. These planes are fast and powerful. Many can go faster than the speed of sound. And all carry lots of weapons. They can fire large guns and missiles.

EARLY FIGHTERS

The first fighter pilots flew during World War I (1914–1918). Back then, airplanes were slower and smaller. Military planes began using jet engines in the 1940s. These engines helped planes become bigger and faster.

Germany's Me 262 Schwalbe was the first fighter powered by jet engines.

Pilots sit in a jet's cockpit. It contains many tools. They help pilots control the plane. Radar is one example. It scans the land and sky. It helps pilots find and shoot targets.

Many fighters use stealth technology. It helps them hide from enemy radar. The F-22 Raptor is a stealth jet. It has flat sides and sharp edges. This shape tricks enemy radar. It makes the signals bounce away. Then enemies don't know where the plane is.

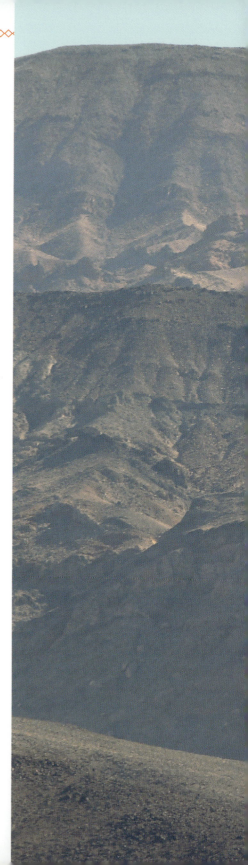

Many stealth jets use dark paint. The paint helps them not be seen by radar.

An F-16 Fighting Falcon has a top speed of 1,500 miles per hour (2,410 km/h).

The F-16 Fighting Falcon is a popular fighter jet. Pilots from more than 20 countries fly it. The jet can fly hundreds of miles without stopping. And it's made to work in all kinds of weather. Pilots can shoot targets even if they can't see well.

PAST AND PRESENT

The F-16 was created in the 1970s. Over time, scientists kept improving it. They updated its radar and weapons systems. That helped pilots see and hit targets. The cockpit got updates, too. New tools made the jet easier to control.

Fighters are built to attack. Pilots often battle enemy planes. But they do other types of missions as well. They may shoot targets on the ground. Or they may protect other aircraft.

OTHER PILOTS

For some missions, fighter jets team up with other aircraft. Militaries include several kinds of pilots. Some fly planes for rescue missions. Some spy on enemies. Others fly helicopters or bombers.

Fighter jets may fly near bombers during missions. They watch for enemy aircraft.

Chapter 3
AIR TO AIR

Many fighter pilots fly in air-to-air missions. They try to shoot down enemy aircraft. Fights between planes are called dogfights. Pilots plan some attacks. Other times, enemy planes surprise them.

If attacked, a pilot may release flares. The flares' heat and light make it harder for missiles to find the plane.

Some dogfights are high-speed chases. Pilots speed after and shoot at enemy planes. In other dogfights, pilots on both sides attack. Jets circle or face one another. They try to find the right angle to shoot.

ACES

Pilots who have shot down at least five enemy aircraft are called aces. People first used the term in World War I. Becoming an ace is not common. The last US fighter pilot to do it fought in the Vietnam War (1954–1975).

The United States used the F-8 Crusader during the Vietnam War.

During fights, pilots often make sharp turns or dives. They may flip or spin, too. These moves help with attacks and defense. One example is the barrel roll. To do it, a plane spins while flying forward. This move makes the plane harder for enemies to hit. It can also help the pilot slow down before shooting.

BLUE ANGELS

The Blue Angels are a group of US Navy pilots. Instead of fighting, they put on shows. Large audiences come to watch. The pilots show off their jets' high speeds. And they do flashy tricks.

The Blue Angels fly F/A-18 Super Hornet jets.

23

Sometimes, planes fight in pairs. A pilot may keep watch for a partner. Or one plane may distract an enemy while the other attacks. Other battles involve large groups of airplanes. The planes may fly in patterns called formations. They work together to attack and defend.

BIG BATTLES

Many battles in World War II (1939–1945) included multiple planes. Sometimes, dozens of planes fought one another at once. The Battle of Britain is a famous example. It took place in 1940. British fighter pilots helped bring down German planes.

The Spitfire was one of the quickest British fighters during World War II.

Fighter jets may have to fly long distances. So, they carry thousands of pounds of fuel. Some jets can fly thousands of miles without stopping. That helps pilots carry out missions far from their bases.

Russia's Su-57 Felon can travel more than 2,100 miles (3,400 km) without stopping.

AIRCRAFT CARRIERS

Navy pilots often launch from aircraft carriers. These huge ships have runways where planes can take off or land. Planes may have dogfights over the ocean. Or they may fly toward shore and fight over land.

Story Spotlight

DOWNING DRONES

In 2024, Iran and Israel were fighting. One night, Iran sent hundreds of drones and missiles toward Israel. Fighter pilots from the US Air Force joined Israeli forces to stop the attack.

The pilots fired missiles at the first drones. The drones exploded. But more followed. For hours, the pilots fired again and again. They ran out of missiles. But they didn't stop. Instead, the pilots used guns to shoot drones. They stopped nearly all of Iran's weapons.

US fighters, such as the F-15E Strike Eagle, helped shoot down 80 drones aimed at Israel.

Chapter 4
AIR TO GROUND

For some missions, fighters attack targets on the ground. Pilots fly toward a target. As they get close, they swoop down. They shoot the target, then keep flying. This is called an air-to-ground attack.

The F-15K Slam Eagle can carry up to 12 MK-82 bombs. Each of these bombs weighs 500 pounds (227 kg).

Some missiles are long-range. Pilots can shoot them from thousands of feet up. But for other attacks, pilots must fly down close. They risk being shot by enemy defenses. To stay safe, pilots try to stay hidden. They may fly low to avoid enemy radar. Radar and sensors also help them watch out for attacks.

GREAT RADAR

Fighter pilots fly F-15E Strike Eagles for some air-to-ground missions. These jets have powerful radar. It can show targets from very high up. It can also show many details about the shape of the ground. This helps pilots fly safely at low heights.

Flying very low makes jets harder for radar to spot. But it also increases their risk of crashing.

Some air-to-ground missions target enemy forces. Pilots may shoot at tanks or soldiers from above. Missions may also attack enemy bases. Bases often store ships, planes, weapons, and supplies. Fighters try to destroy these things. Then enemies can't use them to fight.

One air base may store hundreds of aircraft.

GROUNDED

Air bases are places where military planes take off and land. Soldiers fix and store planes at them, too. Fighter attacks may try to damage a base's runways. Then planes can't take off.

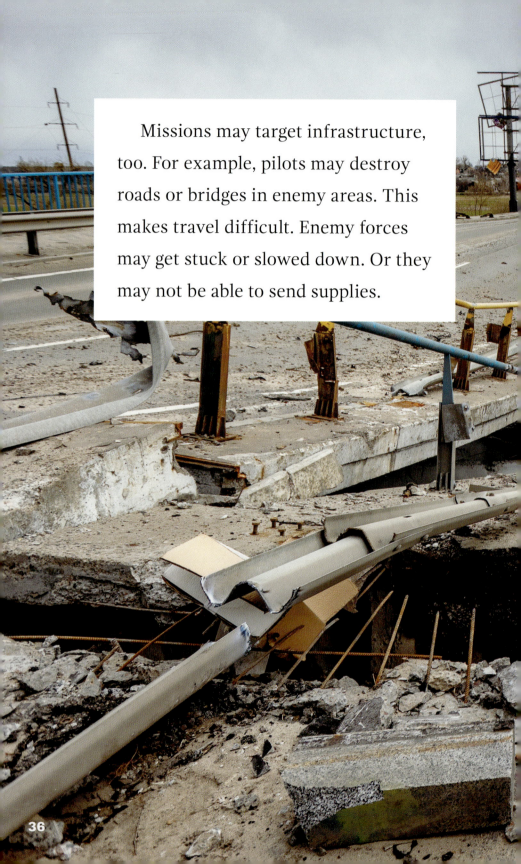

Missions may target infrastructure, too. For example, pilots may destroy roads or bridges in enemy areas. This makes travel difficult. Enemy forces may get stuck or slowed down. Or they may not be able to send supplies.

In the 2020s, Russia invaded Ukraine. Ukraine's military destroyed bridges to slow Russia's attack.

Some radar systems can be moved to different locations. Large trucks carry them.

Pilots may destroy enemy buildings. They may target places that store weapons. Or they may try to damage enemy radar. Pilots may damage factories, too. Then enemies can't make more supplies. All these attacks make it harder for enemies to fight.

AIR ATTACKS

In the 2010s, a group called the Houthis took over much of Yemen. In 2023, the Houthis began targeting Israel. The United States and United Kingdom support Israel. So, they sent ships and fighter jets to attack Houthi targets. They bombed radar, factories, and weapons.

39

Story Spotlight

DESERT STORM

In 1991, the US military helped plan Operation Desert Storm. This campaign was part of the Persian Gulf War (1990–1991). This war began when Iraq invaded Kuwait. Several countries helped Kuwait fight back. They tried to weaken Iraq's forces.

Fighter pilots were a key part of the plans. They flew over Iraq and Kuwait. They shot Iraq's planes and infrastructure. Iraq tried to fight back. But it lost nearly one-third of its forces.

The US military sent hundreds of planes to Iraq during Operation Desert Storm.

Chapter 5
RISKS AND CHALLENGES

Fighter pilots often fly into enemy areas. They risk being shot at. And during battles, many pilots fire at once. If pilots are not careful, they may hit planes on their own side rather than hitting enemies.

Being a fighter pilot is one of the riskiest jobs in the military.

A jet that flies very fast may create a vapor cone. This cloud of water droplets forms around the jet.

Pilots turn, dive, and fly high to avoid being shot. These moves are risky. Pilots often change speed or direction very quickly. This creates forces known as G's.

High levels of G's make it hard for people's hearts to pump blood. As a result, pilots struggle to see and think. They may even black out. They can crash or lose control.

Pilots learn ways to limit the effects of high G's. Before flights, they work out and drink water. During flights, pilots wear G-suits. The suits put pressure on pilots' lower bodies. Pilots also learn ways to breathe and tense their muscles. Both help keep blood flowing to people's heads. But some G's get too high for these things to help.

TOO MANY G'S

In 2018, a pilot was practicing moves for a fighter jet show. He tried to do a looping trick. But he blacked out from high G's. His plane started to fall. One second before he reached the ground, he woke up. But it was too late. The jet crashed, and the pilot died.

Fighter pilots wear helmets with masks that provide oxygen.

Crashes can happen for other reasons, too. Parts of a jet can break. Sometimes pilots can fix the problems in the air. Or they can fly back to base. But they don't always make it. Fuel can be a challenge as well. Fighters usually carry enough fuel for just one mission. If things don't go as planned, they may run out.

GETTING OUT

If a plane is going down, pilots may eject from the cockpit. Their seats shoot into the air. Then they parachute down safely. In 2017, a pilot was training in Maryland. A piece in his jet broke. The plane started to fall. So, the pilot ejected. His plane crashed. But he stayed safe.

When pilots eject, small rockets help their seats launch away from the plane.

49

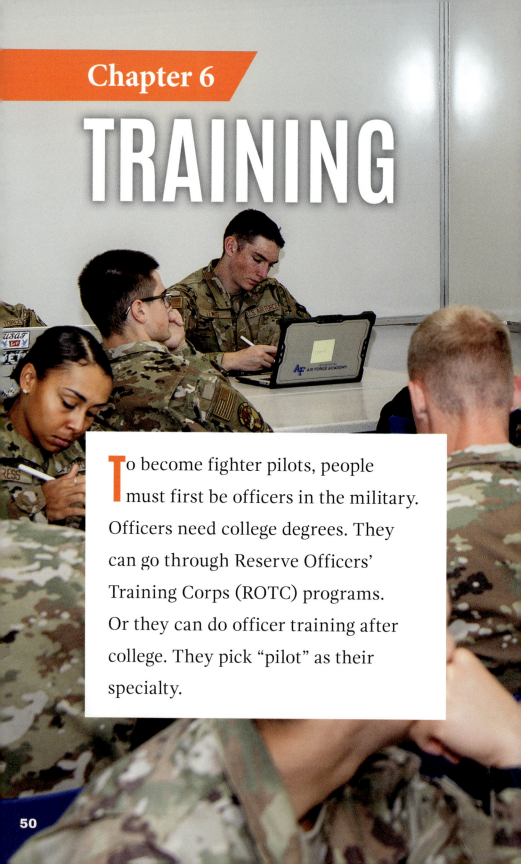

Chapter 6

TRAINING

To become fighter pilots, people must first be officers in the military. Officers need college degrees. They can go through Reserve Officers' Training Corps (ROTC) programs. Or they can do officer training after college. They pick "pilot" as their specialty.

50

To become officers, people go through training programs such as the Air Force Academy.

The next step is flight training. During this step, people take classes. They learn about airplanes and the tools that control them. People also practice flying. They start with simulators. Later, they try flying real planes.

GETTING THEIR WINGS

When pilots finish flight training, they get wing-shaped pins. These pins go on their uniforms. They show each pilot's experience. Pilots can earn new types based on how many years they have served and hours they have flown.

Some flight simulators use virtual reality headsets. They show what flying a plane would look like.

53

Military leaders assign each pilot to one specific type of jet. Then pilots spend time studying that jet. They get lots of practice flying it. They learn every detail of how it works. This training can last a whole year. Then, pilots are ready for missions. Each pilot is matched with a base. Pilots fly out from this place for missions. They may get more training there, too.

Many fighter pilots learn to fly in the T-38 Talon.

Fighter pilots usually spend a few years doing basic missions. Then they may take on more advanced tasks. They may train to use specialized weapons. Or they may help with search-and-rescue. Some pilots become instructors. They teach in training programs.

Fighter pilots often fly in groups called squadrons.

TOPGUN

TOPGUN is an elite school for fighter pilots. The US Navy runs it. Extremely skilled pilots apply to the school. If they get in, they study new dogfighting and air-to-ground moves. Then they go back to their bases. They teach other pilots what they learned. That helps all Navy fighter pilots build skills.

✓ SKILLS CHECKLIST

- Being brave and calm when facing danger

- Completing flight training for fighter jets

- Having very good eyesight

- Staying physically fit

- Thinking quickly under pressure

- Understanding the science of how airplanes work

COMPREHENSION QUESTIONS

Write your answers on a separate piece of paper.

1. Write a few sentences explaining one type of mission that fighter pilots do.

2. Would you want to fly a fighter jet? Why or why not?

3. What is the first step in becoming a pilot?
   - A. becoming an officer in the military
   - B. completing flight training
   - C. using a simulator to practice flying

4. Why would blacking out cause a pilot to crash?
   - A. The pilot would stop controlling the plane.
   - B. The pilot would fall out of the plane.
   - C. The plane's fuel would run out.

5. What does **formations** mean in this book?

   *Other battles involve large groups of airplanes. The planes may fly in patterns called **formations**.*

       A. times when planes cannot fly
       B. groups of planes that fly together
       C. places where only one plane can land

6. What does **launch** mean in this book?

   *Navy pilots often **launch** from aircraft carriers. These huge ships have runways where planes can take off or land.*

       A. crash into the ground
       B. fly up into the air
       C. get hit by weapons

Answer key on page 64.

GLOSSARY

bases
Places used by the military to train, house, and send out troops. Bases also store vehicles and supplies.

campaign
A plan made by military leaders to fight part of a war.

drones
Aircraft that people control from far away or that work on their own. Some drones release weapons.

elite
The best of the best.

exhaust
Hot air and gases that are released by an engine.

infrastructure
The structures, such as roads and bridges, that a city or other area needs to function.

missile
An object that is shot or launched as a weapon.

officers
People in the military who are trained to teach and lead others.

radar
A system that sends out radio waves to locate objects.

sensors
Tools that take in information, such as sounds or movement.

simulators
Devices that copy what it is like to fly airplanes. Pilots use them to train.

TO LEARN MORE

BOOKS

McKinney, Donna. *F-22 Raptor.* Bellwether Media, 2024.

McKinney, Donna. *The United States Air Force.* Bellwether Media, 2025.

Ringstad, Arnold. *US Air Force Equipment and Vehicles.* Abdo Publishing, 2022.

ONLINE RESOURCES

Visit **www.apexeditions.com** to find links and resources related to this title.

ABOUT THE AUTHOR

Trudy Becker lives in Minneapolis, Minnesota. She likes exploring new places and loves anything involving books.

INDEX

aces, 21
aircraft, 16–17, 18, 21, 27
air force, 9, 28
air-to-ground missions, 16, 30, 33–34, 57
attacks, 16, 18, 20, 22, 24, 28, 30, 32, 34–35, 39

bases, 26, 34–35, 48, 54, 57
battles, 16, 24–25, 42
Blue Angels, 22

cockpit, 12, 15, 48
crashing, 45–46, 48

dogfights, 18, 20, 27, 57
drones, 28

formations, 24

infrastructure, 36, 40

jet engines, 7, 10

missiles, 7, 10, 28, 32
missions, 16–17, 18, 26, 30, 33–34, 36, 48, 54, 56
moves, 22, 45–46, 57

navy, 9, 22, 27, 57

Operation Desert Storm, 40

radar, 4, 12, 15, 32–33, 39

speed, 10, 20, 22, 45

targets, 7, 12, 15–16, 30, 33–34, 36, 39

Vietnam War, 21

weapons, 7, 10, 15, 28, 34, 39, 56
World War I, 10, 21
World War II, 25

ANSWER KEY:
1. Answers will vary; 2. Answers will vary; 3. A; 4. A; 5. B; 6. B

64